Peter Søren

Peter's
Torchon Lace

Akacia

Peter's Torchon Lace
By Peter Sørensen

© 2005 Forlaget Akacia
Skovvænget 1
5690 Tommerup
Denmark
akacia@akacia.dk

Printed at Dardedze Holografija, Riga
Second print 2008

ISBN: 978-87-7847-087-4

Introduction

Torchon lace is probably the most well-known and well-loved type of bobbin lace.

The characteristics of Torchon lace are that you only work in one direction – towards yourself. The elements in the patterns are mainly geometric, occasionally forming flower motifs.
You start with x number of bobbins – it could easily be several hundred – and with these bobbins you work both open and more dense grounds. The same bobbins work between elements and grounds, it is only in exceptional circumstances you might need to add or remove a pair or two.

Torchon lace has also become one of my favourites.

I have worked with bobbin lace since 1989, where I got hold of a book about it – and then time just disappeared. Later I went on several courses and in 1991 I began to teach myself. Teaching has provided me with many challenges and a great deal of joy. Throughout the years I have designed for my students, and they have encouraged me to collect these 17 patterns into a book.

Large Torchon patterns leaves lots of ends to get ris of. I have tried to deal with this problem partly through design and partly in the method used for finishing off.

The first part of the book contains runners with a large number of bobbins, then runners joined along the middle and then finally runners worked in strips using only 18 – 20 pairs.

Some special techniques have been used.

"Finishing with a plait (1 pair at each pin)" and "Fininhing with leaves and stalk with buttonhole stitch". Both are described at the beginning of the book.

Everyone with knowledge of bobbin lace making can work these runners. Don't let the leaves and tallies scare you – have a go, because practise makes perfect!

Enjoy yourselves

Peter Sørensen
Agersted, February 2005

Colour code

———— Blue = Cloth stitch, whole stitch (CTC)
———— Green = Half stitch (CT)
———— Red = Cloth stitch with a twist (CTCT)
———— Black = Twist – plait – gimp – dots
√ Sewing
✳ Backstitch

Start with pairs hung open

The pair above the pin is the worker.

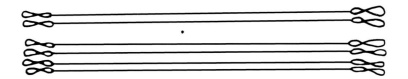

Starting with a plait or a fan

It is advisable to start with two pins to make sewing out easier.

Starting with half stitch

To start with half stitch, hang two pairs on the top pin, twist,
* half stitch, remove the pin and replace it below the treads,
half stitch *, then hang one pair on each pin at both sides as
shown on the drawing. Repeat from * to *.

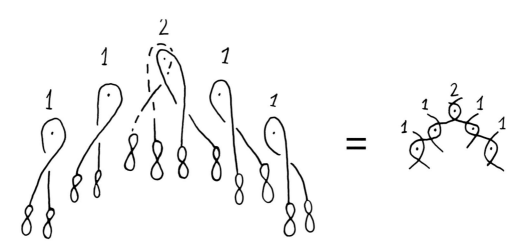

Backstitch

= using the same pin twice

Twist the pair which comes out of the corner
twice, take it behind the pin and bring it back into
the lace with a cloth stitch and twist. This is used
for the runners worked in stripes.

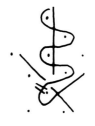

Tally

Start with 2 twists on both pairs.
Weave 8 - 10 times and end with 2 twists.

Finishing with a plait
1 pair at each pin

Sew in all the pairs at the starting pins.

Add 3 twists to the starting pair, then 4 x TC with pair no. 2.

Add a new pair by working a cloth stitch through the plait. Loose a pair on the left side of the plait. Repeat.

To complete the plait, finish with two buttonhole stitches.

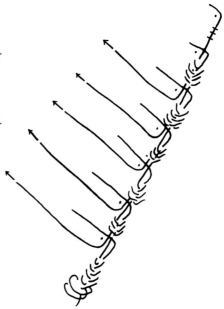

Finishing with a plait
2 pairs at each pin

All the pairs are sewn out – resulting 4 treads at each pin. Work a half stitch at each pin.

Start with 4 x TC.
When new pairs are added into the plait: There are 2 pairs at the pin – 1 is used in the plait – the other is tied off with 1 bobbin from each side of the plait forming a reef knot on top of the plait (the dotted line). Repeat.
To complete the plait, finish with two buttonhole stitches.

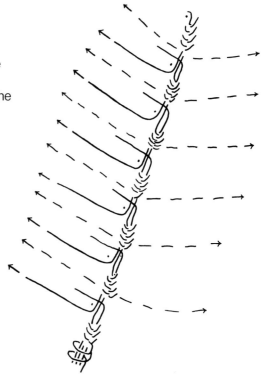

Buttonhole stitch
used for ending a plait etc.

Take one of the treads from the plait, wrap it around the plait and pass it through the loop (see drawing) and pull tight.

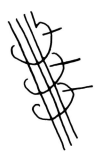

Finishing
with leaves and buttonhole stitches

Sew every pair into the appropriate starting pin.

Use the 2 pairs closest to the middle, work a little plait, and sew it into a pin in the ground. Work a leaf to the correct length and lay it on top of the plait (1). Then work towards the corner.
Use one of the treads for buttonhole stitches. "New" pairs (pairs which still need finishing off) are added when appropriate. Make leaves on top of the stalk as you work towards the corner. If there are too many treads in the stalk you can work a leaf (2) and let pairs "disappear" that way.

If you want the treads to come back into the stalk (3) you work leaf – plait – leaf and then the pairs join the stalk again or you can work a plait and a leaf and place the leaf on top of the plait, letting the pairs rejoin the stalk.
I always finish with 3 or 5 leaves in the corner.

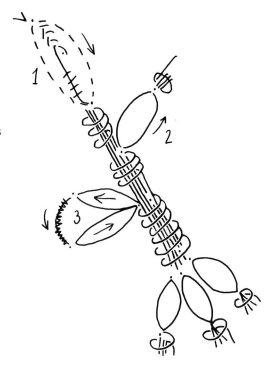

Miss. Blossom
Runner with tallies

35 pairs linen 28/2 (Goldschild Nel 50/3 (green label) can be used)
2 pairs with double tread
1 gimp pair

This runner is sewn in down the middle.
Start as shown on the diagram.
The ground is half stitch with a twist.
On the outer edge you have 2 pairs with double tread. They are worked in cloth stitch (the 2 pairs act as one pair) and you work cloth stitch with a twist and the pin is placed inside 2 pairs (foot side).
The tallies are surrounded by half stitches.
The blocks are cloth stitch.
Before making a sewing, work cloth stitch with 2 twists.
The twists shown at the beginning of the diagram apply for the entire piece.
You can complete the runner by using the "Finishing in a plait with 1 pair at each pin." See page 6

Remember: Enlarge the pricking. Set the copier at 135%

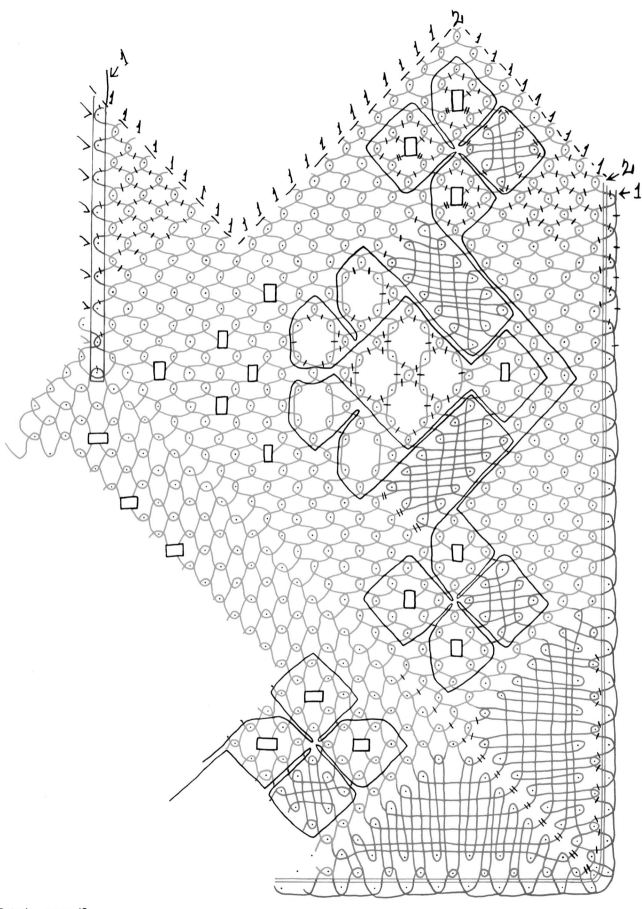

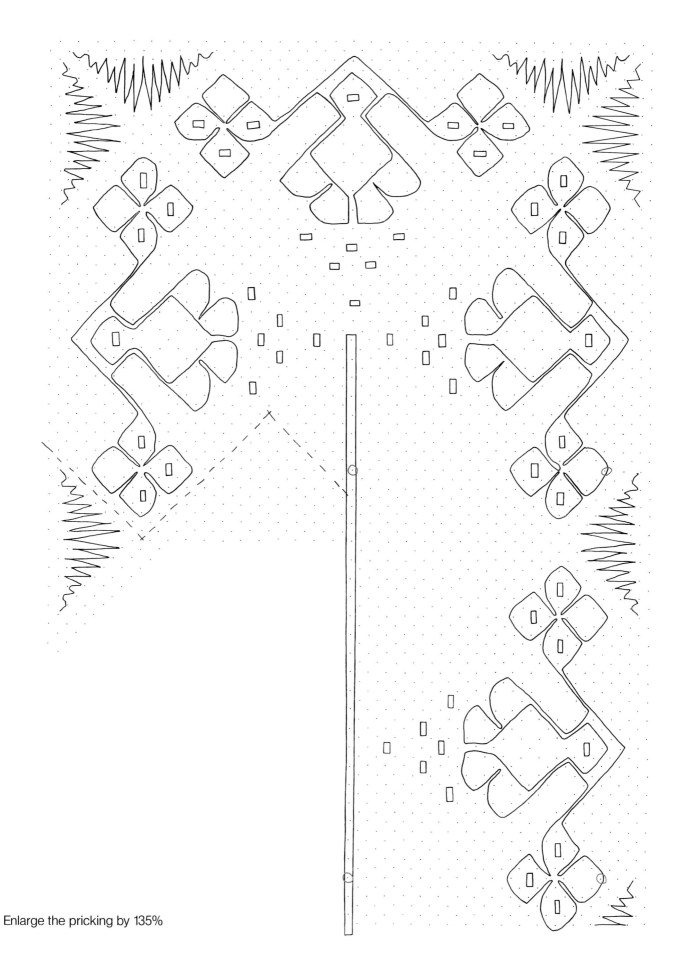

Enlarge the pricking by 135%

Miss Grey
Runner with tallies

36 pairs linen 28/2 (Goldschild Nel 50/3 (green label) can be used)
1½ gimp pairs

This runner is sewn in along the middle.
Start as shown on the diagram.
The fan is cloth stitch, with cloth stitch and a twist on the outside edge.
The ground and the honeycomb are worked in half stitch with an extra twist.
The triangles and the small hearts are cloth stitch.
The inner pair for making sewings in the center is worked in cloth stitch with 2 twists.
The twists shown at the beginning of the diagram apply for the entire piece.
You can complete the runner by using the "Finishing in a plait with 1 pair at each pin." See page 6.

Remember: Enlarge the pricking. Set the copier at 160%

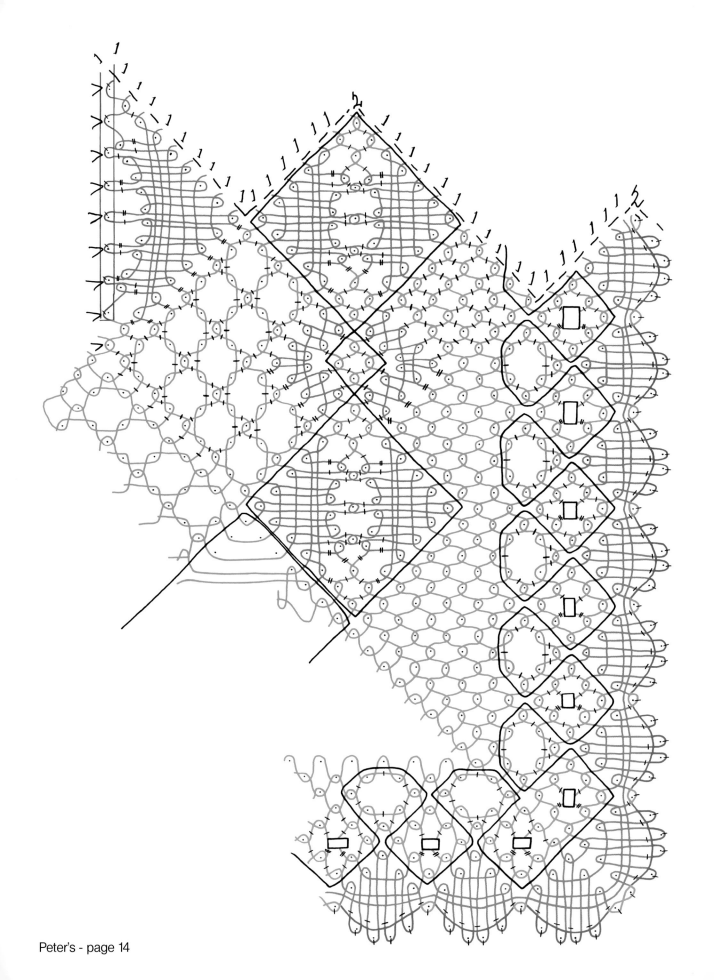

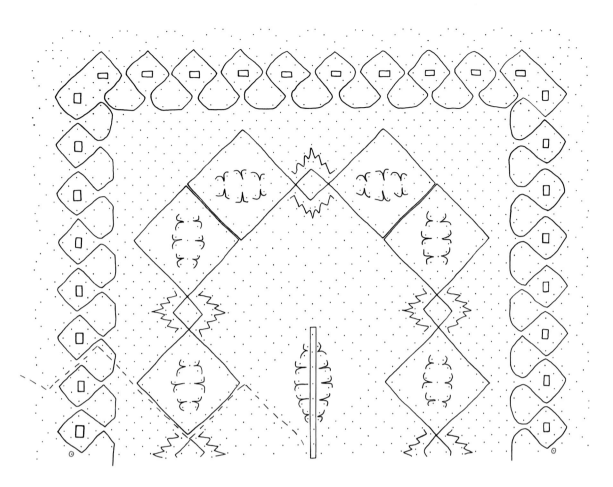

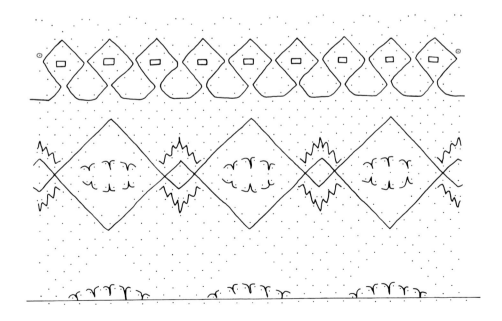

Enlarge the pricking by 160%

Miss Sanne
Runner

86 pairs linen 28/2 (Goldschild Nel 50/3 (green label) can be used)
5 gimp pairs

Start as shown on the diagram.
Start with pairs hung open (page 4).
The fan is cloth stitch, with cloth stitch and a twist in the outside edge.
The honeycomb is worked in half stitch with an extra twist.
The blocks are cloth stitch.
The spiders are cloth stitch surrounded by half stitch.
The twists shown at the beginning of the diagram apply for the entire piece.
Sew in and end the work.
You can complete the runner by using the "Finishing in a plait with 2 pairs at each pin."
Tie off to complete the work.

Remember: Enlarge the pricking. Set the copier at 180%

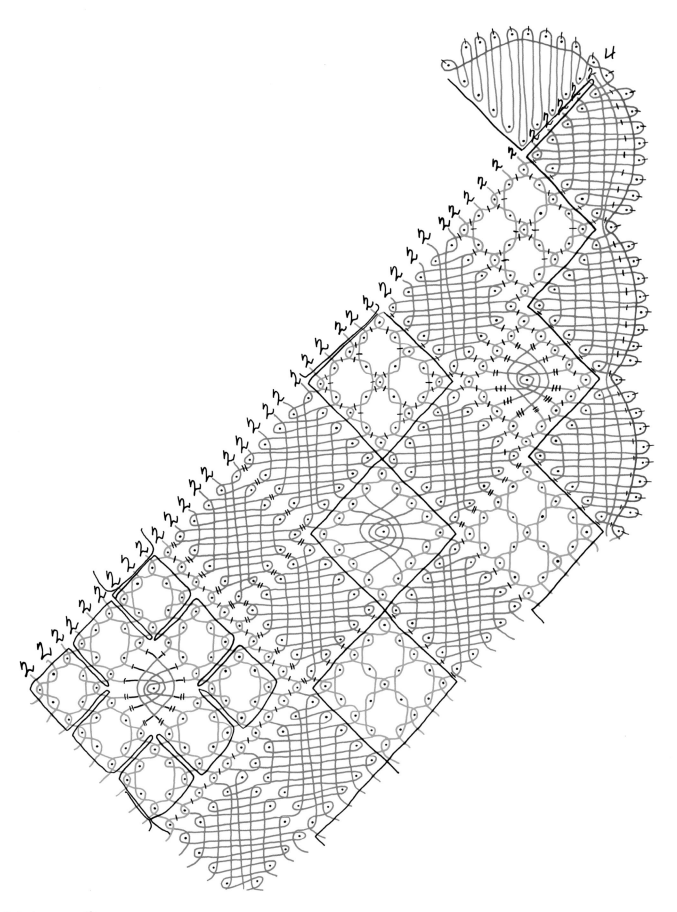

Enlarge the pricking by 180%

Miss Mette
Runner

68 pairs linen 28/2 (Goldschild Nel 50/3 (green label) can be used)

Start with hanging pairs open.
The fan is cloth stitch, with cloth stitch and a twist in the outside edge.
The narrow zigzag is worked in half stitch.
The snowflakes are worked in cloth stitch.
The honeycomb is worked in half stitch with an extra twist.
The twists shown at the beginning of the diagram apply for the entire piece.
To finish you sewn out and tie off or complete the work by using "Finishing with a plait_2 pairs at each pin" (page 7).

Remember: Enlarge the pricking. Set the copier at 120%

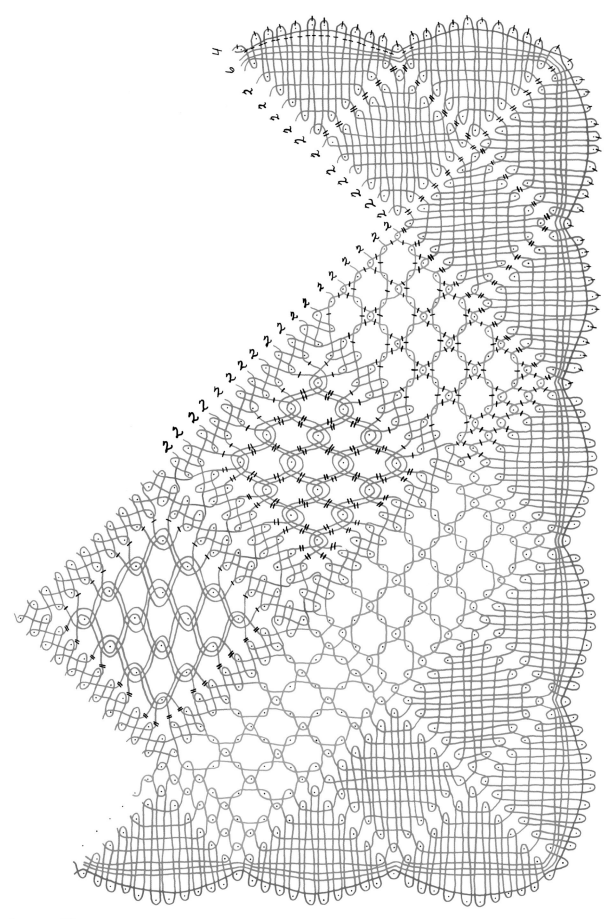

Enlarge the pricking by 120%

Miss Green
Runner

24 pairs linen 28/2 (Goldschild Nel 50/3 (green label) can be used)
3 gimp pairs

Start at * with 3 pairs and follow the diagram.

The ground is half stitch with an extra twist.
The outer edge is cloth stitch with a twist and pin inside 2 pairs.
Block 1 is cloth stitch. As block 2 you can choose between A, B, C, D or E. (B is used on the photo.)
The fan is cloth stitch with cloth stitch and a twist on the outer edge and the pin is placed inside 2 pairs (foot side).
Sew in along the middle.
The twists shown at the beginning of the diagram apply for the entire piece.
The ending can be worked with a plait.

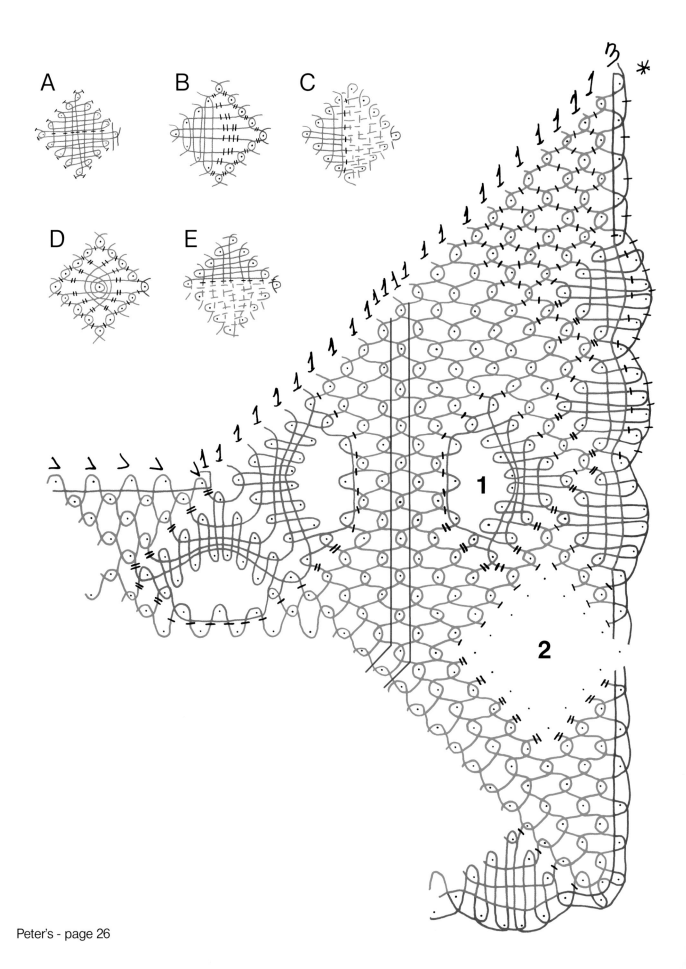

A   B   C

D   E

1

2

*3

Miss Rita
Runner with a fringe

148 bobbins (74 pairs) linen 28/2 (Goldschild Nel 50/3 (green label) can be used)
5 gimp pairs

As you start with a fringe, you need 4 bobbins (not wound in pairs) at each pin. Measure how long you want the fringe to be and make a knot and put the pin in the knot before tightening.
The outer edge is worked with cloth stitch with a twist, the pin placed inside 2 pairs (footside).
The ground is half stitch with an extra twist.
The zigzag stripes and the triangles are cloth stitch.
The honeycomb and the block with the honeycomb sides are half stitch.
The twists shown at the beginning of the diagram apply for the entire piece.

Remember: Enlarge the pricking. Set the copier at 105%

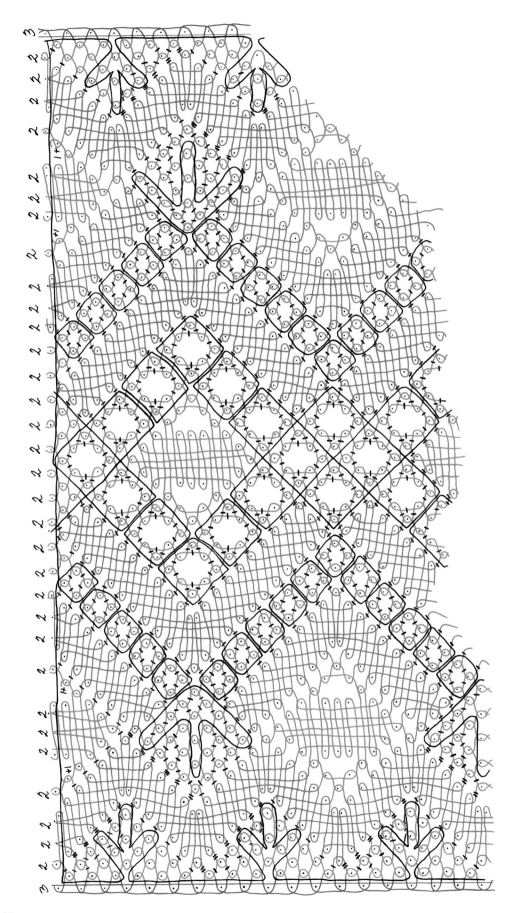

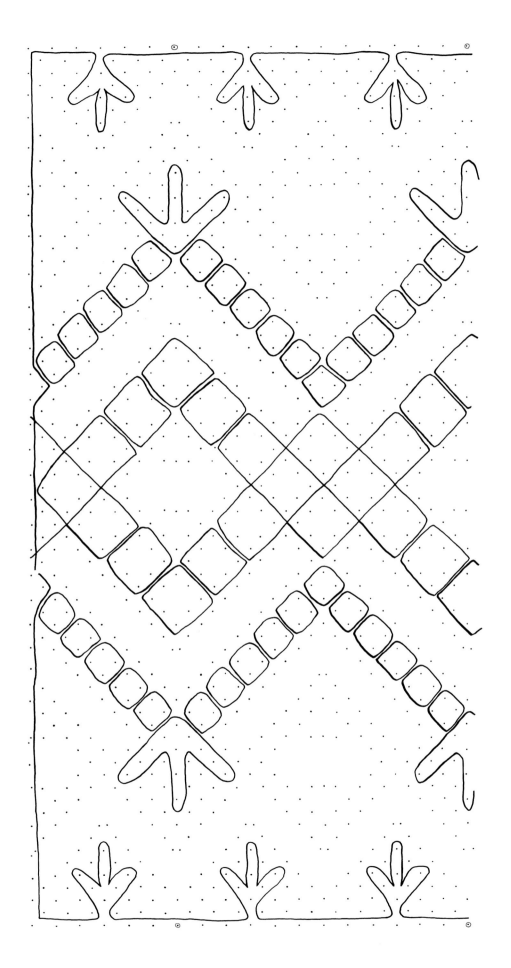

Enlarge the pricking by 105%

Miss Leaves
Runner with tallies and leaves, worked in strips

25 pairs linen 28/2 (Goldschild Nel 50/3 (green label) can be used)
1 gimp pair

Start with the leaves. Look carefully at the small diagrams. Add 2 more pairs, plait with 1 of the pairs – the other is used when you return to that point. A pair is then added at +.
1 pair is added at the left side of the lace at +, this is here worked in cloth with a twist.
On the outer edge a pair is added at +.
On the outer edge work cloth with a twist, pin inside 2 pairs (footside). Those 2 pairs are worked as 1 pair in a windmill crossing and they are also used for the leaves at the edge. 2 pairs are only used for the end pieces (* in the buttom diagram at page 34).
The ground and Honeycomb are both worked in half stitch with an extra twist. On both sides work cloth stitch with a twist.
The twists shown at the beginning of the diagram apply for the entire piece.

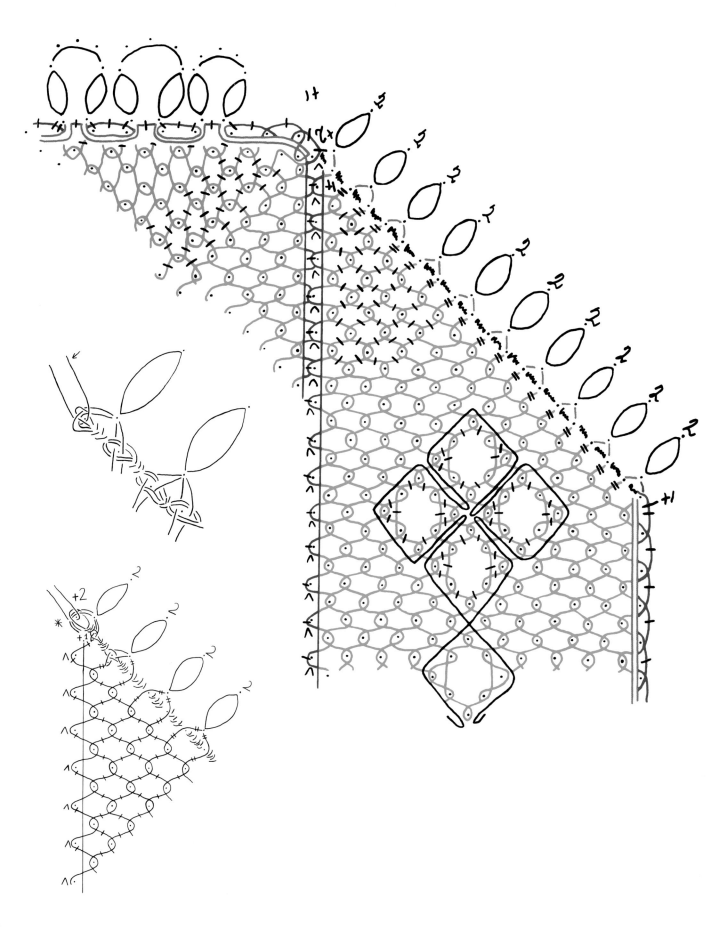

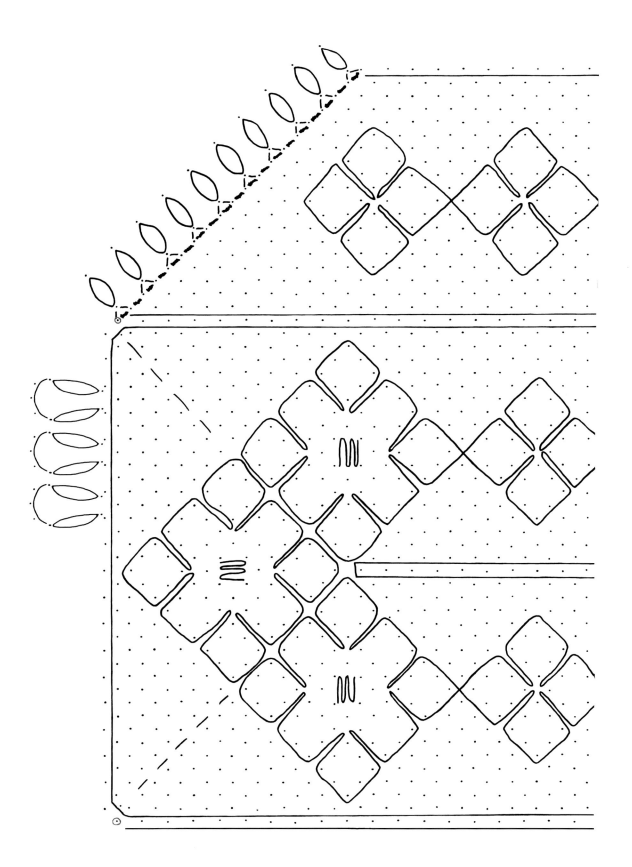

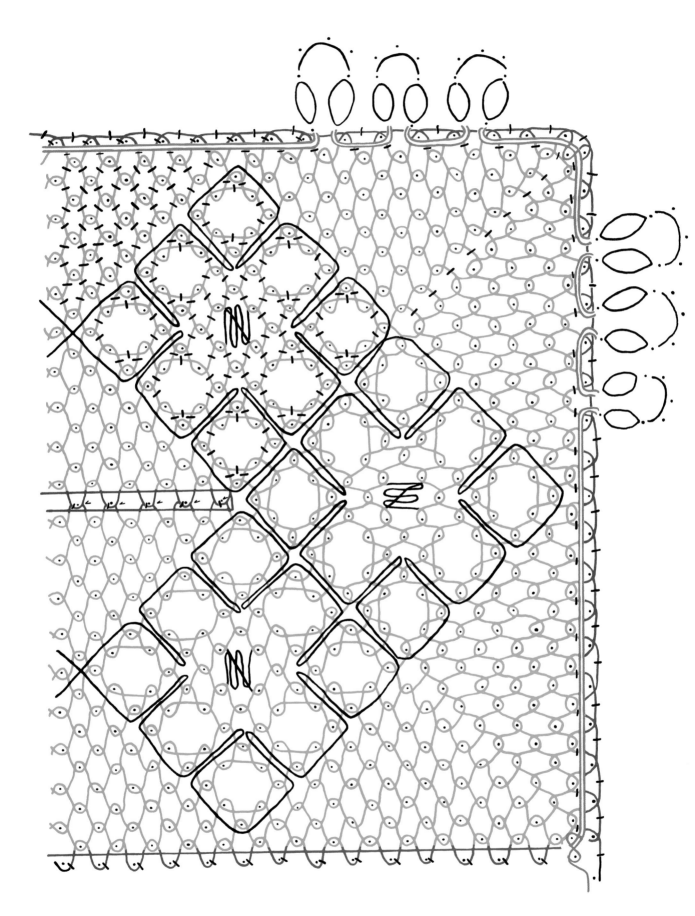

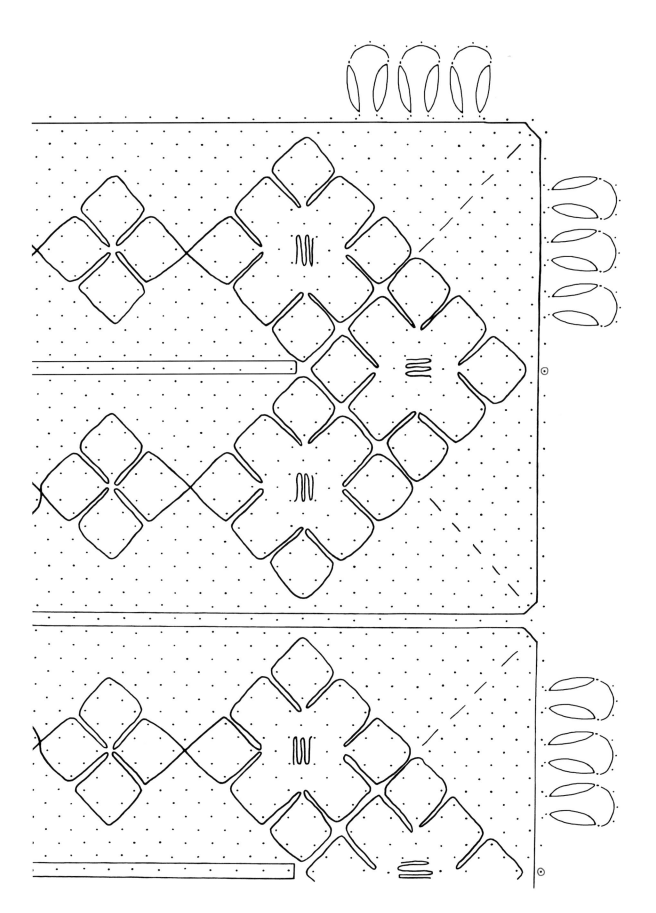

Miss Winter
Runner

66 pairs linen 28/2 (Goldschild Nel 50/3 (green label) can be used)
1½ gimp pairs

The hearts on the outer edge are cloth stitch, with cloth stitch and a twist in the outside edge.
The inner hearts are half stitch.
The ground is half stitch with an extra twist.
The gimp is the most significant part and forms the pattern.
The twists shown at the beginning of the diagram apply for the entire piece.
You can complete the runner by using the "Finishing in a plait with 2 pair at each pin." See page 7.

Remember: Enlarge the pricking. Set the copier at 130%

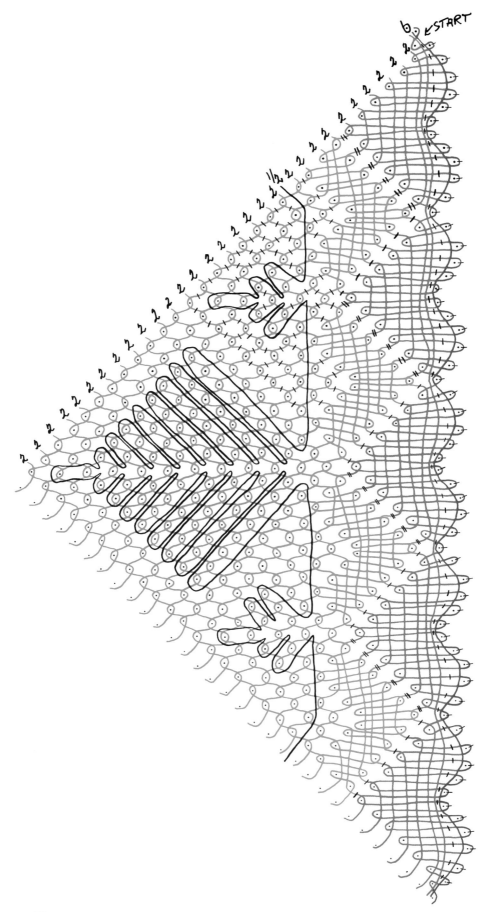

Enlarge the pricking by 130%

Miss Blue
Runner with tallies
- worked in strips

16 pairs linen 28/2 (Goldschild Nel 50/3 (green label) can be used)
1 gimp pair

Begin at * with 3 pairs, 2 are used for the plait and the third is used when you return to that point.
New pairs are added along the plait, and in the end of the plait one pair is used in the edge and the other pair is used in the fan.
The ground is half stitch with an extra twist.
The fan is worked in cloth stitch with a cloth stitch with a twist on the outermost edge.
The honeycomb is half stitch with a twist.
The blocks are cloth stitch.
The triangles in the ends are rose ground in half stitch.
One pair "z" is only used when you work the turns.
Sew in along the middle.
At * and when pair "z" is used you work a backstitch.

Remember: Enlarge the pricking. Set the copier at 150%

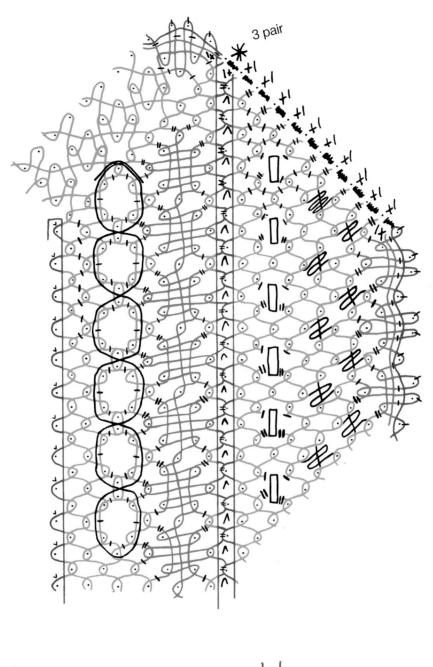

3 pair

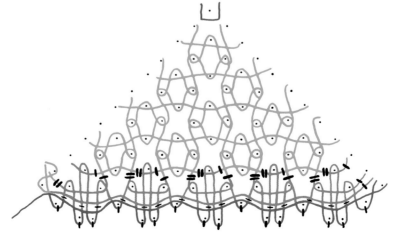

Enlarge the pricking by 150%

Miss Heart
Runner with hearts

39 pairs linen 28/2 (Goldschild Nel 50/3 (green label) can be used)
4½ gimp pairs

Start as show on the diagram.
The hearts are worked in half stitch.
The ground is half stitch with an extra twist.
The fan is cloth stitch with cloth stitch and a twist on the outside.
Sew in along the middle.
The twists shown at the beginning of the diagram apply for the entire piece.
You can finish with a plait.

Remember: Enlarge the pricking. Set the copier at 145%

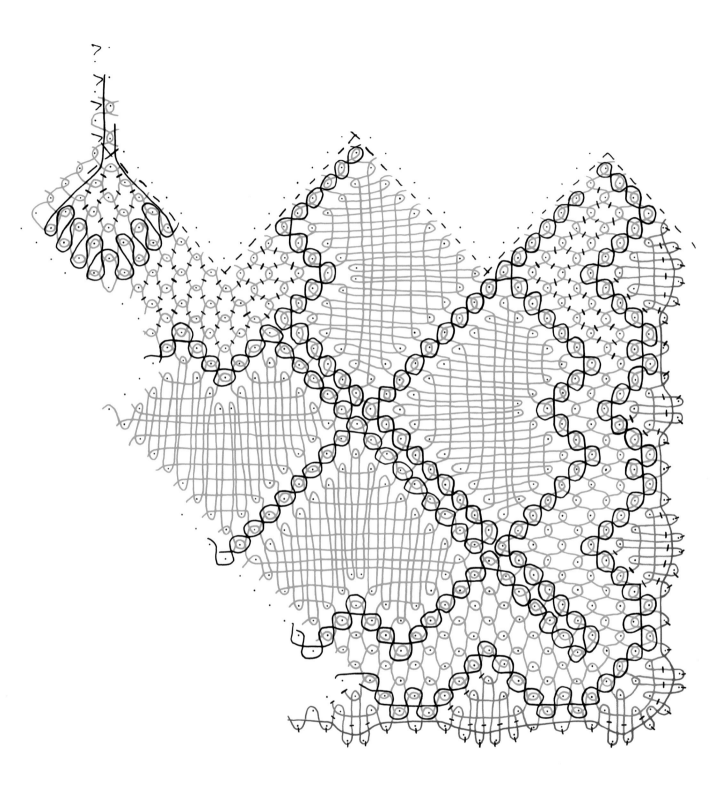

Enlarge the pricking by 145%

Miss Hyacinth
Runner with triangular ground

27 pairs linen 28/2 (Goldschild Nel 50/3 (green label) can be used)

Start as shown on the diagram with 2 pairs plus one extra in the big fan.
The fan is worked in cloth stitch with cloth stitch and a twist on the outer edge.
The stitch between 2 fans is half stitch.
The triangular ground is cloth stitch.
The zigzag is cloth stitch and the stitch between 2 zigzag tapes is half stitch.
The rose ground is half stitch.
Sew in along the middle.
The twists shown at the beginning of the diagram apply for the entire piece.
The finishing can be worked with a plait.

Remember: Enlarge the pricking. Set the copier at 140%

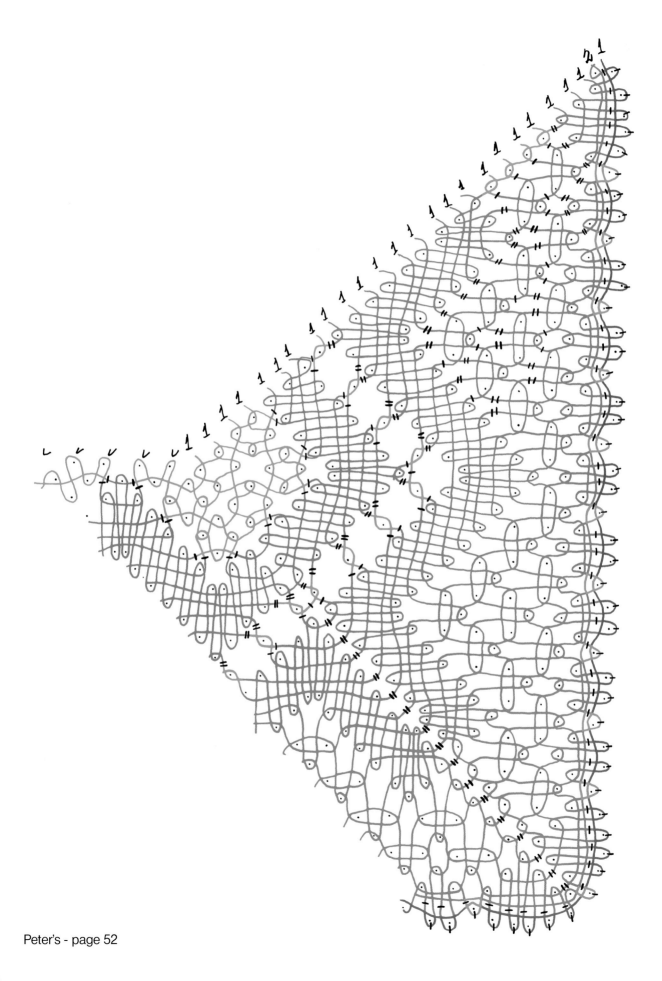

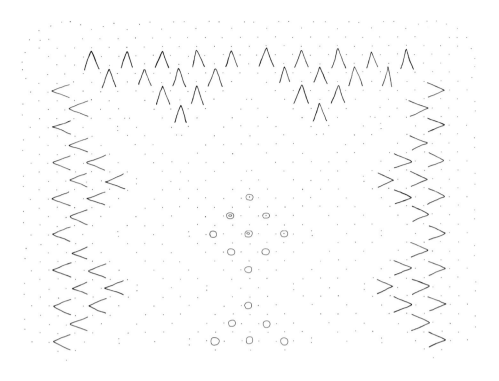

Enlarge the pricking by 140%

Miss Orange
Runner with zigzag and honeycomb

27 pairs linen 28/2 (Goldschild Nel 50/3 (green label) can be used)

Start as shown on the diagram with 3 pairs in cloth stitch with a twist.
The triangles are cloth stitch and the outer edge is cloth stitch with a twist and pin inside 2 pairs (foot side).
One of the zigzag stripes is worked in half stitch and the other in cloth stitch.
The ground is half stitch.
The small triangle towards the middle is cloth stitch.
Sew in along the middle.
The twists shown at the beginning of the diagram apply for the entire piece.
The finishing can be worked with a plait.

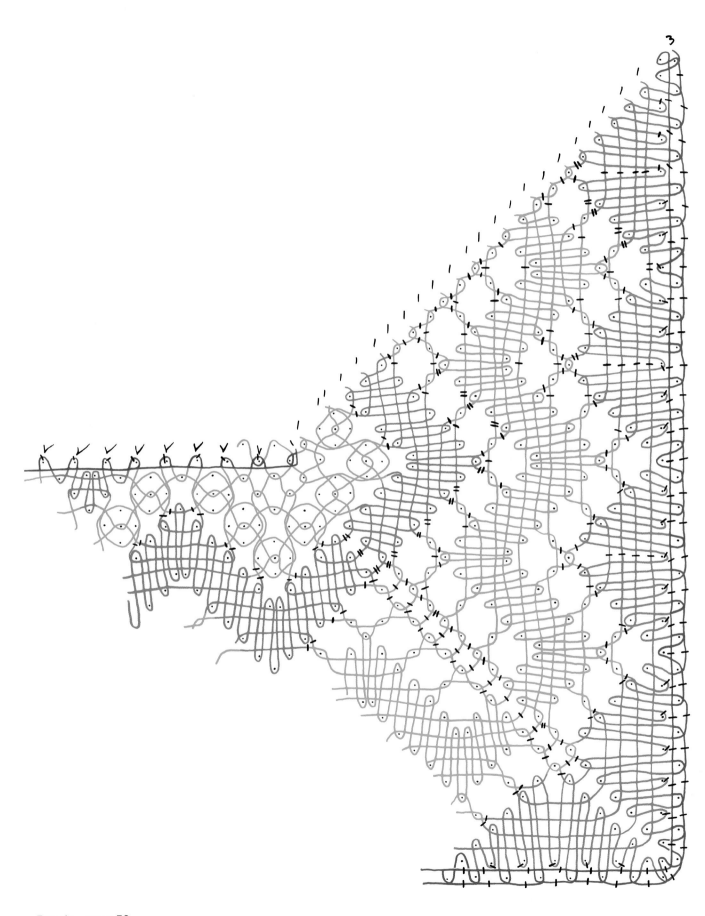

3

Miss Silver
Runner worked in strips

16 pairs linen 28/2 (Goldschild Nel 50/3 (green label) can be used)
1 gimp pair

Begin at * with 3 pairs, 2 are used for the plait and the third is used
when you return to that point.
New pairs are added along the plait, and in the end of the plait one
pair is used in the ground and the other pair is used in the edge.
The ground is half stitch with an extra twist.
The fan is worked in cloth stitch with a cloth stitch with a twist on
the outside edge.
The honeycomb is half stitch with a twist.
The stars are worked alternately in cloth stitch and half stitch.
When the triangle in the turn is worked, one pair is left out until the
next turn at that end when it is worked in a backstitch.
See diagram

Remember: Enlarge the pricking. Set the copier at 120%

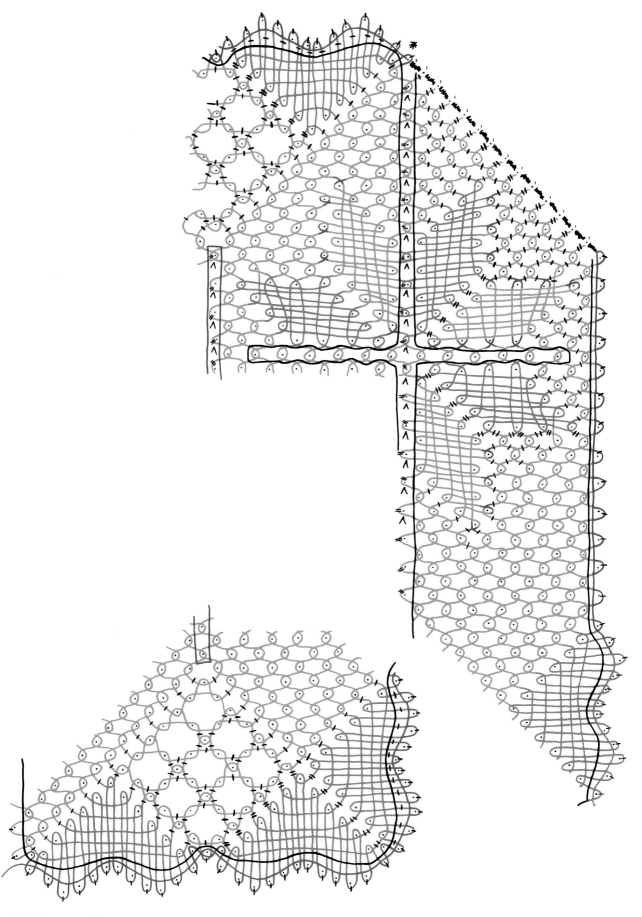

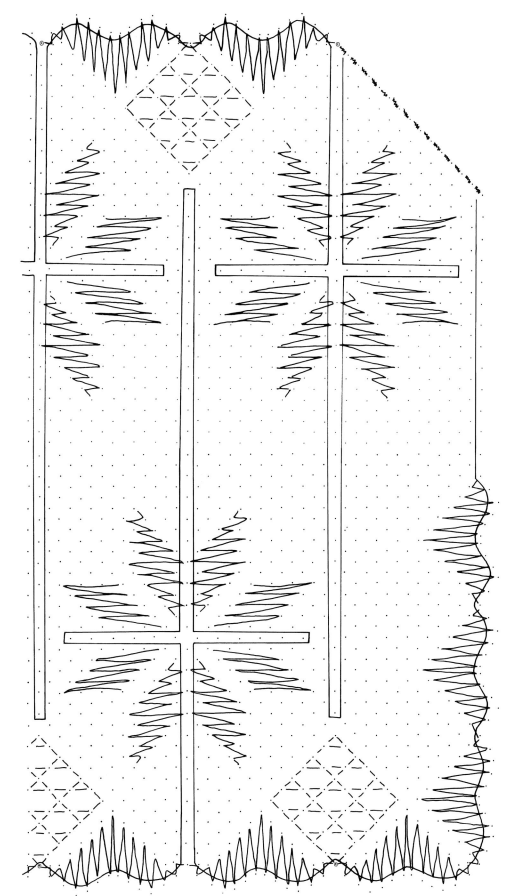

Enlarge the pricking by 120%

Miss Star

Christmas runner
-with stars in half stitch

29 pairs linen 28/2 (Goldschild Nel 50/3 (green label) can be used)
1 gimp pair

Start as shown on the diagram.
The ground is half stitch with an extra twist
The heart fan is half stitch with 2 cloth stitch with a twist on the outside edge. Pin inside 2 pairs.
The star is half stitch.
Sew in along the middle.
The twists shown at the beginning of the diagram apply for the entire piece.
You can finish with leaves and buttonhole stitches (see page 7).

Remember: Enlarge the pricking. Set the copier at 120%

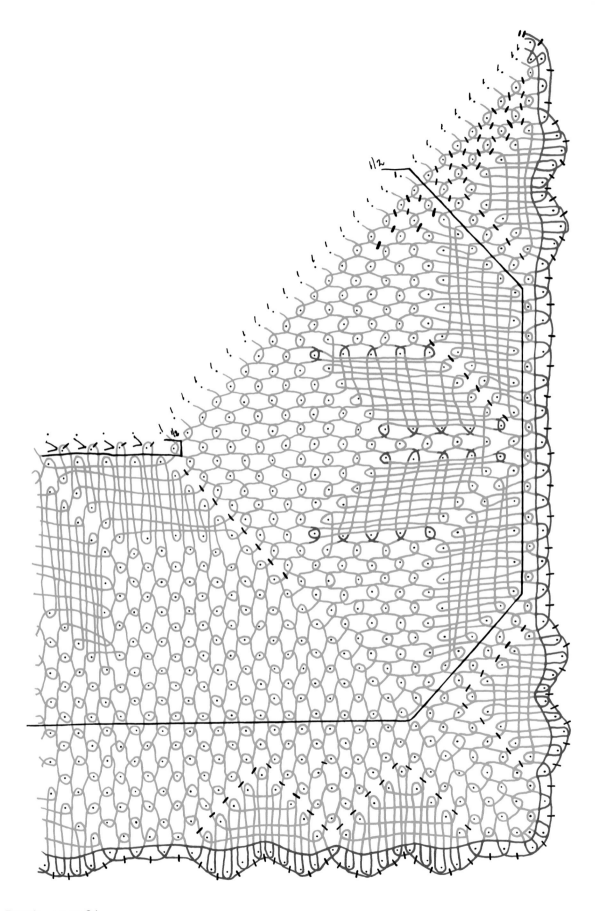

1/2

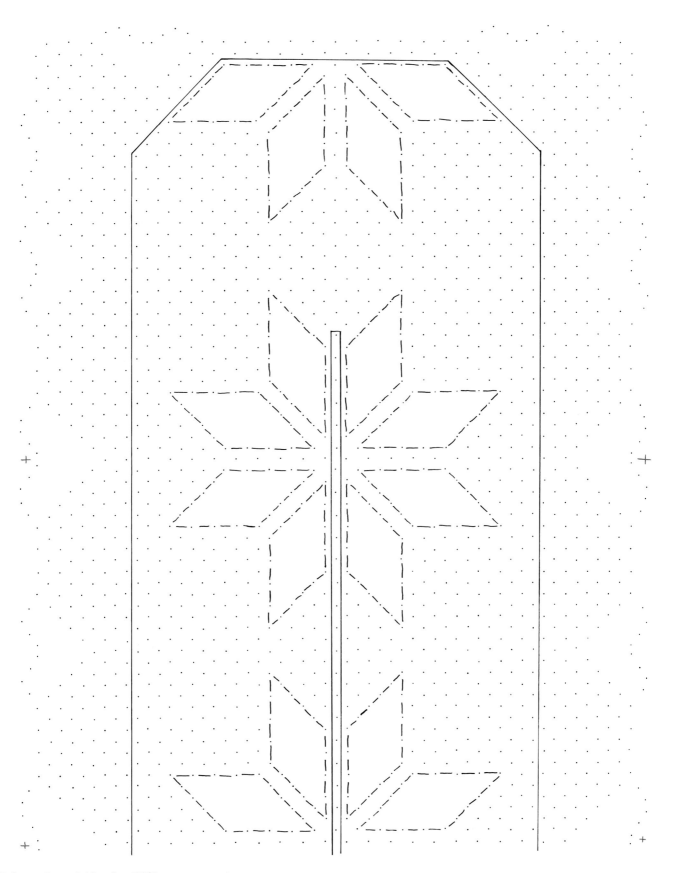

Enlarge the pricking by 120%

Miss Rosa
Runner

80 pairs linen 28/2 (Goldschild Nel 50/3 (green label) can be used)
2 gimp pairs

Start by hanging pairs open and work the small fans in cloth stitch with cloth stitch and a twist on the outside edge.
On the diagonal sides one pair is added on the inside at each pin. It is worked in half stitch with cloth stitch and a twist on the outer edge.
The ground is worked in half stitch with an extra twist.
The triangles in the middle are half stitch with cloth stitch and a twist where the 2 pairs meet.
The tallies are surrounded by half stitch.
The twists shown at the beginning of the diagram apply for the entire piece.
You can complete the work by using "Finishing with a plait, 1 pairs at each pin" (page 6).

Remember: Enlarge the pricking. Set the copier at 120%

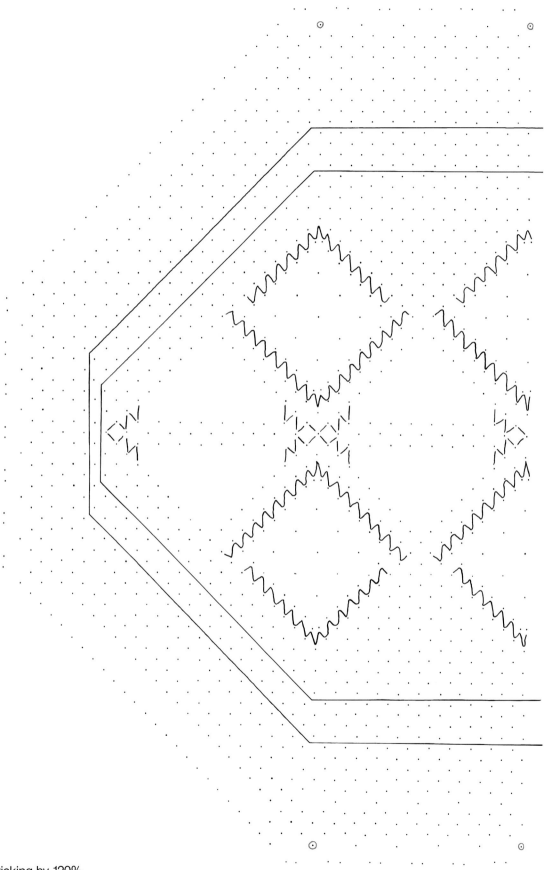

Enlarge the pricking by 120%

Miss Heidi
Runner

42 pairs linen 28/2 (Goldschild Nel 50/3 (green label) can be used)
2 gimp pairs
5 gimp bobbins

This runner is sewn in along the middle.
Start as shown on the diagram.
The fan is worked in cloth stitch with cloth stitch and a twist on the outermost edge.
The ground and honeycomb are worked in half stitch with an extra twist.
The zigzag tape is cloth stitch.
The twists shown at the beginning of the diagram apply for the entire piece.
You can complete the work by using "Finishing with a plait, 1 pairs at each pin" (page 6).
When you have finished the runner you could thread a silk ribbon along the middle to hide the sewings. (See photo)

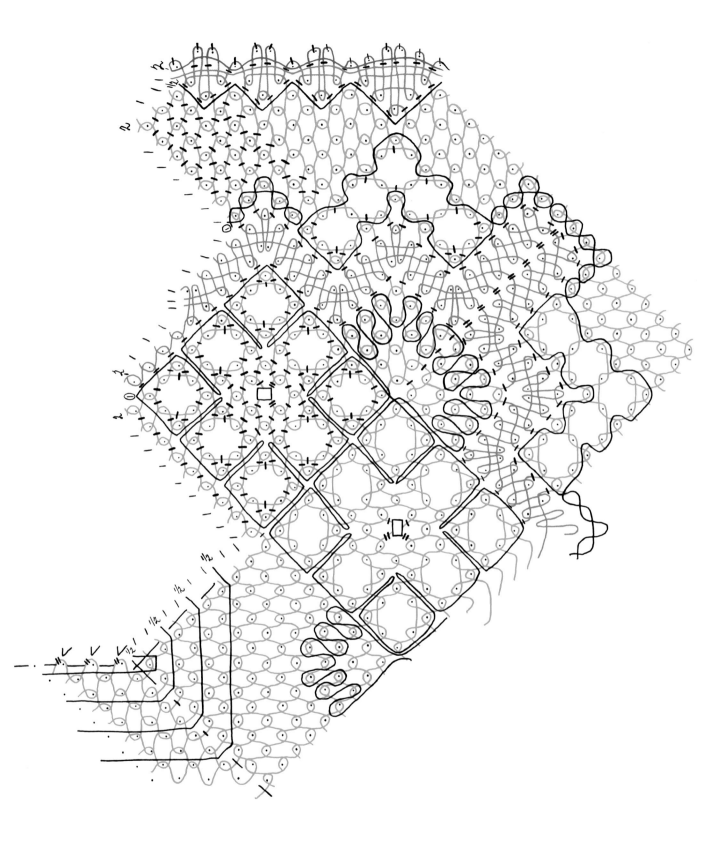

Miss Purple
Runner

42 pairs linen 28/2 (Goldschild Nel 50/3 (green label) can be used)
6 gimp pairs

Start as shown on the diagram.
The zigzag is worked in cloth stitch; the rose ground is worked in half stitch.
The ground is half stitch with an extra twist.
The fan is cloth stitch, with cloth stitch and a twist on the outside edge.
The outer edge is cloth stitch with a twist and pin inside 2 pairs (foot side).
Sew in along the middle.
The twists shown at the beginning of the diagram apply for the entire piece.
The finishing can be worked with a plait.

Remember: Enlarge the pricking. Set the copier at 125%

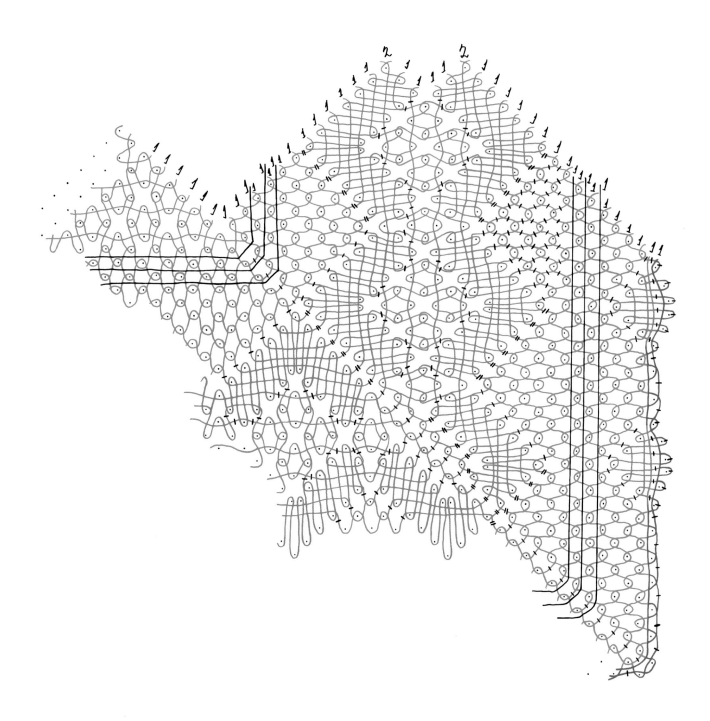

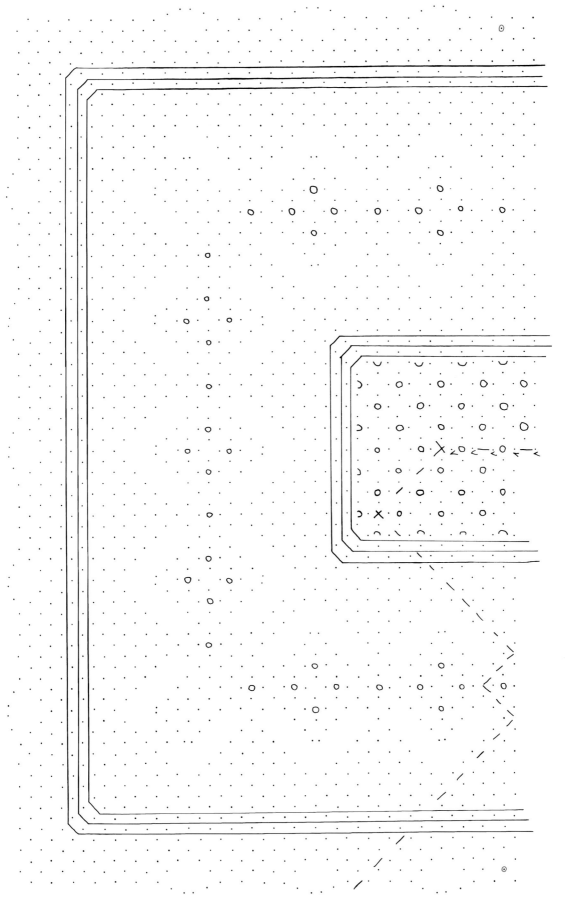

Enlarge the pricking by 125%

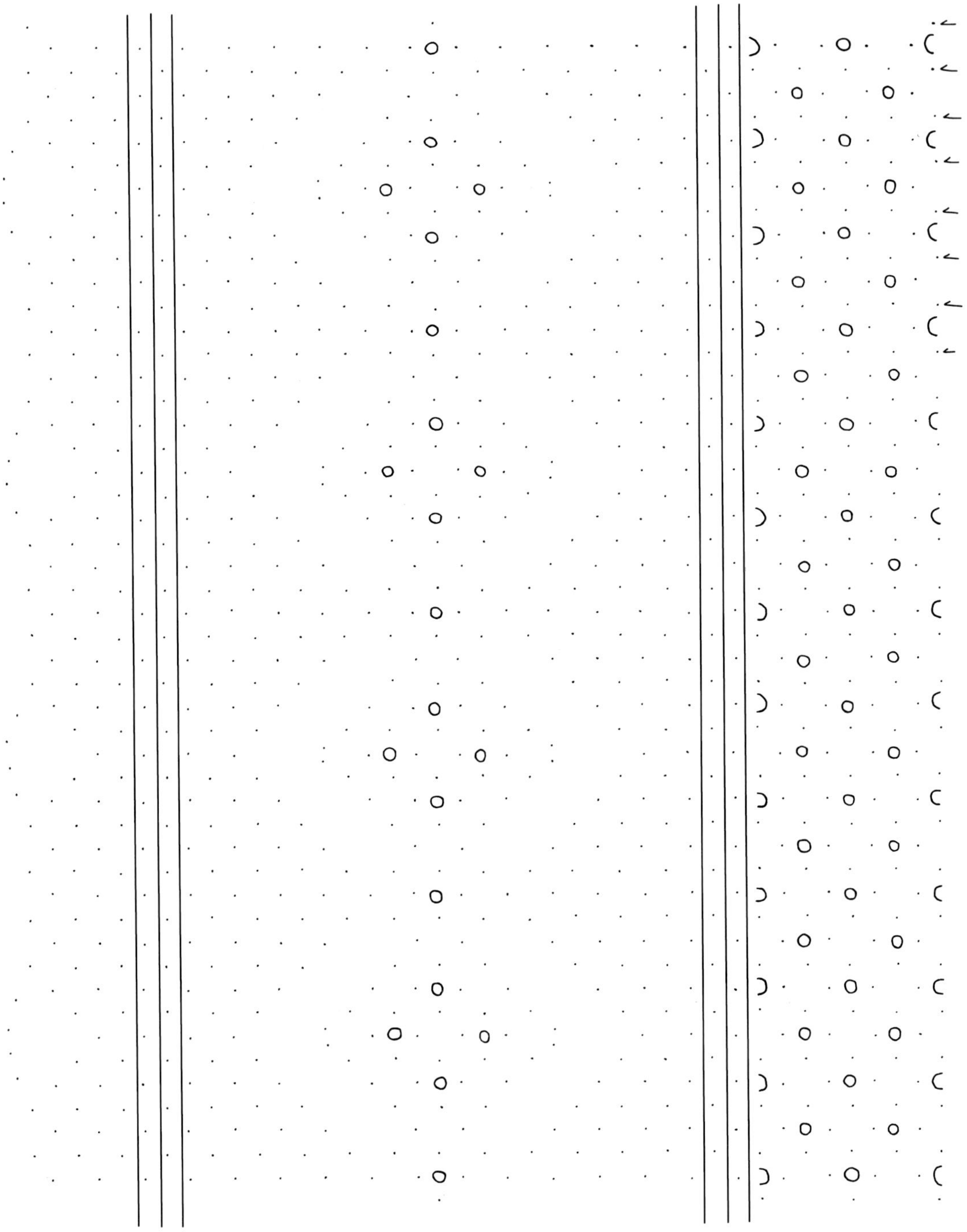